Echoes
of
Silence

Echoes
of
Silence

Finding Your Voice

Polly Prose

Copyright © 2024 Polly Prose

The characters and events portrayed in the poetry are fictitious. Any similarity to real persons, living or dead, is coincidental and not intended by the author.

No part of this collection of poetry may be reproduced, or stored in a retrieval system, or transmitted in any form or by any means, electronic, mechanical, photocopying, recording, or otherwise, without express written permission of the author.

All rights reserved, including the right to reproduce this book or portions thereof in any form whatsoever.

Interior design by Polly Prose
Front and back cover by Polly Prose

Paperback ISBN 978-87-975141-0-8
eBook ISBN 978-87-975141-1-5

Published by LRP Svendsen

♥♥♥ *To all those trying to find their voice in a world that is filled with unnecessary noise.* ♥♥♥

The Poetry Digest

And more surprises…

This is the first book of three in the Finding Yourself Series, a collection of poetry that addresses subjects such as anxiety, self-doubt, and the road to finding your voice. As some of the poems were originally written as slam poetry it can add extra depth to read them out loud to feel the rhythmic beat of the puns and prose play together.

In whichever way you decide to read, I hope you enjoy and feel the effects of the words originally intended.

Enjoy the journey!

No More Control

Facing your own bully

It's hard to explain
Hard to recognize
The paralyzing pain
That crowds my insides.
I've craved recognition
To the point of addiction
Craved love;
Sort of.
Desired acceptance
Without reflectance
From you
From the masses.

But each time
With a demeaning remark
It hits the dark
A cynical laugh
Pitying look
Embarrassed shake of your head,
My soul shrivels
I try to be civil
A tiny piece of me dies
Amongst all the lies.

Each time another crack
Into my heart is hacked.
It breaks
And it aches
Shatters.
Creating splatters.
From the darkest pits
I'm out of my wits

But I have a choice to make:
Continue to break
Or glue the pieces back.

Am I up for the task?
Can I shed the mask?
Two options, both
Painful
Awful
Distressing for a fact.
I have to commit
So I can benefit
One piece at a time
The hard road I will climb.
I am okay.
I am worthy.
I won't take your lies anymore
Never again like before.

I have friends
That love me
Appreciate me.
Accept me.
Every single piece
Break
Shard
Part
It is who I am!

And piece by piece
A long-desired peace I reach
I appreciate myself.

Break by break
Whatever it will take
I accept myself.
And with every step I take
I start to love myself fully
As I face my own bully
I let go of the hurt
And leave it in the dirt.

The pain
Ingrained in my brain
The demeaning remark
That you bark.
I let go of you
It was so overdue.
You have no more control
And I've reached my goal.
In my own life I am the lead
And my heart no longer
will continue to bleed.

Finding Clarity

Standing your ground

It was a long road for me
And so many mistakes were made
The lesson learned was the key
And I am thankful despite being burnt
- Being played.

On many occasions you were
right there
Not knowing exactly why,
It wasn't all that clear
And for way too long I waited
To ask the right question
With discretion
To get feedback
To repair the never-ending crack.

You looked at me with surprise
Like I was the one out of line.
Honestly, it was fine.
I simply tried to be authentic and true
Seeking an answer
To gain some clarity to the insanity.

And as time passed
The deeper I fell
- I know you could tell -
It felt out of my control
And it took a toll.
With sweet words and flattery
Disguised emotional battery
I was caught in the net of deception.
Well, that was at least *my* perception.

I guess that's when I turned a blind eye
As I thought you were my true ally.
The uncertainty of it all was
so messed up
But I couldn't just stop.
I was innocent
I was ignorant
I learned my lesson
in the most brutal way –
It certainly was no child's play.

You looked at me with surprise
Like I was the one out of line.
Honestly, it was fine.
I simply tried to be authentic and true
Seeking an answer
To gain some clarity to the insanity.

And as soon as I poured out
my heart to you
- A floodgate waiting to be opened -
You just knew.
Your stony-faced frown
Told me instantly to back down.
You were far from happy
And became a bit snappy
For what I had to convey
To my own dismay.

But the load on my back was lightened
And brightened,
And the hope I had lost was regained

Unrestrained.
With ecstatic relief I
Finally found my clarity in all that
Senseless insanity.
I prayed for you to understand
The 'heart-to-heart' at hand
Not reprimand.
You shouldn't have judged,
Not even a smudge
As I needed to share
To see if you would care
Thus, to clear the air.
But you couldn't see it
And that was the key
To the fullest degree
You needed me too -
In my point of view.

Looking back, I have no regrets
Despite all the distinct distress
There is only joy and relief
And now, finally, I am able to breathe.
With a cheerful smile
And a happy sigh
To the past
And to you
I say goodbye.

Rage on the Rising

Tapping into a different vibe

It starts with a slight simmer.
The mood growing dimmer
And not a glimmer of hope
or a shimmer
Of anything reassuring for comfort -
Only impatience
A touch of annoyance lurks around.

You huff and you puff
Everything becomes rough
As your irritation rises.
Your soul agonizes
Turning into refined indignation.
The simmering bubbles
are allowed to rise,
Expanding to resentment,
Discontentment.
Displeasure
At your own leisure
You dwell on,
And face fearlessly - head-on.

Pressure builds up
Without any let up.
It intensifies
Amplifies
Multiplies.
Stronger and stronger
It surges,
Melting into rage
Stewing and brewing
under the surface.

You don't let it out
And it continues to rise high
Touching the top of the sky
And then - you are close to tears.
You start to cry.

You keep it in.
Hidden
From the world.
From yourself?
You plaster on a smile
While your *character* is put on trial.
Words relentlessly stab at you
Slashing through your interior
Making you feel inferior.
It wears you out
There's no doubt.

Then pressure builds up, up, up
To the top of the highest peaks
Within your own body
Making you feel groggy -
And a bit foggy.
Anger turns into rage
At this stage.
People surprised that you have
A temper
A voice
A say
An opinion,
That you're not
somebody else's minion.

No more!
No longer, 'cause you are
so much stronger.
The surprise
At the demise
Of their perception of you.
Stunned
Shocked
Mystified.
It cannot be denied.

Anger and outrage
Boil over
Due to overexposure of
Hate
Animosity
Unkindness.
You blow up in their faces
Leaving devastation and places.
Burn bridges
Shatter the past
With a big blast.
You stop caring
Start swearing
Tearing up your insides -
Declaring you're okay.
But there's no way.
Those you've left in your wake
When you break and shake
At the ache,
From the hurt

The stabs of the words
Slashing you to pieces.

It takes time to heal
To feel,
Again.
But you can.
All you need is to let out the steam
And never stop to dream.
And once in a while maybe scream
To yet again find that gleam
In your eyes,
Shedding the demoralizing disguise.

Little by little the anger will subside
And you no longer will need it to hide.
With love and kindness
You take a stand
And you yourself defend
Not giving in to every
single command.

They will all learn
What it is you yearn
And how you can burn at every turn.
You will let go of the anger
And learn to speak with more candor.
You'll release the frustration
The indignation at every station.
You'll be proud
To be loud
Happy for your own views

That amuse and *you* choose.
You'll let go of the rage
building up inside
'Cause you're on one helluva ride.
Well, that's the wise thing to do,
I might add.
But if I may be frank and direct -
At times I just want to be fuming mad!

The Rawness of

Realization

When reality teaches you a lesson

You wake up estranged
Only to realize
That things have changed.
What you knew from before
Is there no more.
For a brief moment you're in a free fall
Grasping onto anything
And everything
Mourning your own downfall.

Confusion overtakes
And you realize the trusty breaks
Are gone
Broken
Demolished.
You cannot stop the change
It will reach you in the end
No matter how much time
you will spend
Reflecting
Deflecting
Projecting
Avoiding reality.

Then it hits you
And the things you knew
Are no longer there
As a reliable guide,
They've been pushed aside.
It's unpleasant
That they are no longer present
Saving you from being swept away

By a landslide of
Empty emotions
Fleeting feelings
And mind-numbing notions.

The rawness hits you hard.
Acceptance is pushed to your limits,
As the shifting shadows
Stop terrorizing your security.
Bitter sweet perception of truth
Brimming on the horizon.
It's raw
It's painful
It's shameful
But a necessary evil of the upheaval.

The rawness of that realization
Hits you hard
Leaves you scarred.
It was needed
And now you can move on
Unimpeded.

Lost in Space

Battling codependency

What do you want?
I've tried to figure it out.
There's always this doubt
Clouding my mind
My thoughts
Inclined
To be defined.
When there's increased mess
Storming up stress
I guess
The turmoil gets lost
Tossed
To the side with a high cost.

I want to know
To fulfill that need
With a good deed
And stop the bleeding
of your heart
Before *you* fall apart.
But I cannot be what you want
Need
Require
Even aspire.
Whatever you desire
Is beyond my ability
I say with true humility.

You have to do the hard work
On your own
Set the tone.
And *I* need to protect

Myself,
Before I get wrecked
In my own way
Becoming yet again prey.

Yet, I have faith
Faith in you
It's true.
You can get through
The zoo
Of emotions and pain
Shed that chain,
That holds you back
To get back on track.
Don't be lost in space
Just continue the race.
Continue to fight
For happiness.
Don't be lost in nothingness.
But it's up to you
As this only *you* can do.

For way too long I have tried
Cried
Died inside
Watching you hurt
In the dirt
Refusing to stand tall.
Needing *you* to be a wall
Strong and sturdy
Much less wordy
Dealing with your own shit

And never quit,
While having a fit.

I've needed you to be calm
Like a soothing balm
Refreshing
Caressing
Not depressing.
I want to help and support
But I always fall short
The reason being clear
 - I need you to hear.

It's not within my power
On this or any hour
(Now this might make you sour).
It truly is in your own hand
To finally take a stand
Take care of you
So you can get through
Whatever it is creating trouble
And enforces your inner struggle.

You will have to battle
Get things to rattle
Take some action
Without distraction.
You need to heal
I appeal.
Can we make a deal?
Do the work
Don't be a jerk.

It's for your own good,
And you know that you should.
So get off your own ass
Of course with some class.
Work off your butt
Cause you're in a rut -
I know it in my gut.

You don't believe me?
What can I say?
You know it's true
You don't have to be blue.
You can heal for you.
You can heal for me
For your family
Un-bashfully.
For us
No time or need to discuss.

I have faith
In the growth
For us both.
In the process, I confess,
I have full confidence
- Without consequence -
That you can be
A great suc-cess!

Change of Perspective

Fighting depression

Today I woke up deciding
Not to let the darkness overtake.
It was gray outside
Gloomy and dreary.
A perfect setting
for a somber state of mind.
I paused for a moment
And gazed into emptiness
Only to realize the wonders
unfolding around me.

Wind, rain, darkness,
The usual suspects,
My mortal enemies.
A pause
A breather
A restart was all it took.
So, I took another look.

My normal nemesis turned into
great assets.
The wind picked up
A slight drizzle dramatized
The shadows of darkness
And the leaves started to dance
in the street
Surrounded by a chain of
unveiled trees.

I'm glad I woke up today.
I'm thankful today was gray.

Confused Mess

Fighting uncertainty

What is it
This continuing confusion
That keeps growing inside
Expanding
Filling every pore
Corner
Crevice
Crack
In my restless mind?

Am I right?
Wrong?
I don't feel strong.
I keep on wavering
This side
That side.
The pressure builds up
It's not something I can stop.
I try
I really do try.
But each time I'm thrown back
Choked by Confusion
Plagued with Puzzlement
Torn apart by Turmoil.

Mess. Mess. Mess.
All this distress.
Why do I not step back?
Why do I not just leave?
I continue to have flashbacks
Grief builds up inside

Confinement
Happens.
I reside to solitude.
I try to ignore this
Dismiss
Avoid pummeling into the abyss
Again
Like before.
I manage
Somehow
The only way I know-how.
Fight.
Fight.
Yes, I fight
That's right.
Right?
I push back
Move forward.
Attack.
Maybe not so callous
So blatant,
With pumped up malice.
No, I fight back with TLC
Answer every plea with glee.
That is what sets you free.

Do not turn to the pitiful state
Of those who hate.
Think of those who suffer and hurt
Who remain on the outskirt
Of the social jungle
Those that easily stumble.

Be ready to help
Someone who calls out
And is too humble
To shout:
"I need you!
I need you.
Please help me."

I guess that's my cue.
I listen carefully
Prayerfully,
To the words that are uttered.
I've been there myself
On the bottom,
Clawing my way to the top
Trying hard not to drop
Back into confusion.

Mess.
The disorderly distress of chaos.
And even though you fall back
Whack!
You may grouch on the couch.
But I'll tell you the trick real quick.
Don't beat yourself up.
It's not the totality
The end
If you bend.
It's just the way things go
At times
Sometimes
Any given time.

That's what I've learned.
The unforeseen occurrences
Give you no reassurances
That things will always work out.
You can rise again.
And again
After falling
Dropping
Crashing.
Another day will start
And you move on
You move forward
Despite being a confused mess.

You welcome the dawn
You refuse to cave
Break
Dig your own grave.
You fight to live.
Give.
You need to thrive
Feel alive.
So that's what you do.
You find your own crew
And together you fight
Despite what might
Transpire.
You light that fire
Inside
With pride
Not mourning the things
that have died.

No, you stand up again.
You make a plan
You learn by trying
Sometimes crying.
Definitely by applying -
It's terrifying.
You apply the lessons
And make great impressions.

You're a Survivor
A Champion
A Warrior
A Fighter.

You rid yourself of any hypocrisy
React always highly carefully.
Show great empathy
And hospitality.
It has rendered others to turn to you
Thankfully.
The mess will be there.
But love the mess
And don't stress.
It's all a part of you.
And the who
You are.

Muzzled with Maturity

Remembering your inner child

Remember that moment as a child
When the whole world was open
and wild
Each time you thought of
becoming older
You knew you would grow bolder
Without a single chip
on your shoulder.
The future was bright,
Exciting,
It was pure delight
Inviting.
Nothing was going to stop you
From making your grand debut
As a legitimate adult
And no way were you going to bolt
From the adventures and
responsibilities
Set before you.

All you saw were possibilities
Capabilities
Options and choices
Alternatives and encouraging voices
Opportunities.
Hopes and dreams
were common friends
Bursting at the seams
But that's not where the story ends.

You had ambition filled with aspiration
That saturated every sensation.

Nothing could stop your vision
As you dreamed about being
a musician
Going against tradition,
A writer because you're a fighter
Who paints with words and phrases
While visiting different places,
And familiarizing yourself with
fascinating faces.

The future was thrilling,
Exhilarating
Astoundingly captivating
As you brainstormed about tomorrow.
No lingering shadow
Hung over your head
Filling your body with dread.
You weren't being naïve
Or living in some make-believe world
You just didn't know how to grieve
As you still believed
you could achieve it all
Creating sparks and avoid
the default option.

And then …

Reality hit you hard
You put up your guard
Became scarred
As troubles started to bombard you
With setbacks

Creating miniature cracks
Into your body and soul -
You lost sight of your goal.
The present became somewhat
Anticlimactic
Traumatic.
You became more pragmatic
Even dramatic and enigmatic.
Everything became more complicated
Less animated
And more calculated.
There was no more room
for spontaneity
As you got bulldozed by reality.

Dreams and imagination
Gave way to fierce frustration
Duty and stability
Paired with liability
Became more important than impulse.
Desire considered barbed wire
A thing you should not try to acquire
A waste of time,
Almost a crime
If you wanted to climb
That social ladder
To be a success
To continue to impress.
All of that should make you happy
And getting your degree
Was a must
So you had to adjust.

Until one day …

You woke up to your own dismay
Realizing that life is devoid
Of games and play
And all your dreams are destroyed.
You try to remember that child
You've reviled and exiled
Who you once use to be
How carefree -
Before your degree -
You were.
How imagination filled each day
Like some riveting mystery play.

Why are we told to grow up
And stop …
Dreaming?
Grow up to be an adult
As part of some idolized cult?
Can we join the two?
Revive that child inside
And show it off with pride
Instead of pushing it aside?

Let's collide the two
Try on a different view.
You can be mature
With allure
Meshed with childlike fascination
It can be your redesigned foundation,
From hardships the grandest vacation.

When we look at the world around
With a dreamlike background
Hope will keep soaring
And life will never be boring.
Blessings and joy will keep pouring
As you keep adoring and exploring
Every single moment - in time.
Don't waste a second on negativity
But embrace both productivity and
creativity.

Then I reckon,
Life will be filled with festivity
And humor at every turn
And lacking exceptional pleasure
- the greatest treasure -
Will never again be of concern.

Fleeting Foundations

Readjusting your expectations

Disappointments
Pour over you uninvited,
Ignited
By a moment.
It's just another component
mixed with Memories
Often caused by your random nemesis,
Stirred with expectations
That all allegations and
Confrontations
Have been erased,
Or displaced.

It leaves a bad aftertaste
In your mouth
When you realize
They're still being hypnotized
Monopolized
Seduced,
Introduced to
Grandiose stories in different
Categories
All designed to entice,
And most certainly to add
spice and flavor
To capture their devoting favor.

You can see the appeal
How it makes them feel
As the authoritative 'lies' being told
Will unfold
Start to congeal

And sound overtly real
And true
Which is why they're now a part of
the *updated* crew -
The inner circle for a purpose.

It's really just déjà vu
As you're yet again being confiscated
Partially obliterated -
But now,
By choice.
There's no room for hope
While you fight to cope
With disappointment
That's flooding your system,
Clouding your personalized wisdom.

Despite your own vote
Seeing them gloat
You feel abandoned
Stunned being shunned
Yet again,
The weak link in the chain
You're made to believe you're
Insane
Lame
A stain on the clique as a whole
That you stole its soul
The purpose, its goal.

You never gave into the illusion
In all the confusion

Refused to be fabricated -
It's just so frickin' complicated.

The sadness overtakes
As our friendship slowly breaks
Deteriorates
Which only indicates
The underlying power
Is still operating
Triangulating
Circulating
And dominating.
It's the behind-the-scene
String pulling by *The Queen.*

Contemplating what to do
While mourning what was
The probable cause
Of being aggrieved
And bereaved
You adjust your expectations
And recognize that everyone has
their own limitations.
We are all harboring internalized
wounds and wrath,
While walking a rocky path
On a journey
That can at intervals be
tragically thorny.

Echoes of Silence

Reading between the lines

Shhh…
Do you hear that?
Right off the bat -
Or did it fall flat?
Wait for it?
Just a bit.

Shhh…
You have to commit
For it to completely transmit.
There!
Right there
Piercing the air
Like a soft spoken prayer.

The sound of silence
The quiet riot
Turning into an art form,
A swarm of peace
Filling every crease
Echoing in space
Leaving no trace -
Of sound.
It's profound!

It's the absence of it
You admit to yourself
That surrounds you
As it breaks through
The barrier
Of your interior walls
Shielding you from

Aggressive calls.

Shhh - Once more!
Just listen
For the stillness
In its illness
Of complete nothingness.
The quiet has its own calm,
A balm
For the stressed soul
With power to console
And make you again whole.

Hush-hush!
Don't rush.
Take a minute
To test your own limit.
Be radiantly mute
And tune in carefully
Listen to the harmony
Of the silent notes
The subtle quotes
Administrating a lethal dose
Of quietude
Adding to the serene mood
Of tranquility
In its fragility.
There's beauty in the complex melody
- Respectively.

You still don't hear it?
The echoes of silence?

It's right there
Penetrating the air
Everywhere
Surrounding you
Crowding your space.
You can't erase
Or displace it
So just openly embrace
The vibrations
Understand the fluctuations
In the non-verbal communications.

Silence is not quiet,
Absolute absence of sound
Cannot be found.
The waves sounding softly
Pulsate magically through the air
Louder than you think
Forcing your heart to tick in sync,
When you momentarily blink.

That is why
I'm not afraid to defy
The notion of being quiet,
The peace with ease
Sheer and utter soundlessness -
The whole idea of the absence
of sound.

That is why
I've never felt at ease
As silence is just a tease,

The calm before the storm
Waiting to perform
The beginning of the end,
There to simply stay still and pretend.
I'm not ashamed to declare
And share -
'Cause it's helped me to repair:

Silence isn't flawless
Providing sound solace.
And to be honest, as promised -
I've always heard
And been stirred by
The thunderous echoes of silence.

The Silent Game

Breaking the silence

I've tried to figure it out
What it's all about
Whether it's just a state of mind
That can be left behind
On its own
Or an actual issue
An enigma
Marked with severe stigma?
Can it be openly spoken of
Measured in some way
When it's not kept on display
When it's hidden from sight
And it looks as if you're doing alright?

Are you ashamed to admit
That the corrosive feeling continues
To hit
Your heart and soul
That it's out of your control
Falling down that black hole
once more
And you try to ignore
That you've lost the war?

The shame turns into a game
Of plastering on a smile
With guile
It becomes hard to reconcile
The two
As the confessions
Leave you open to questions
With aggression

Plunging you back into
deep depression.

You try to explain
What's going on in your brain
Try to contain
And share only a fraction
Of what's in your heart
For a start.
But the chain reaction
Of people's overreaction
Shuts you down
Makes you frown
As you come to understand
Their harsh reception -
Bitter response felt first hand.
In fact, it's only your own perception
That's left to stand.

You fear it's taken as judgment
On their character
A criticism
Of their humanism
Mannerism
Leaving you more lonely than before
And you feel like a sellout
A fraud
Compromising
When you continue smizing
Through it all
Downplaying what you said
By roleplaying

In the midst of the outfall.

It's not about socializing
Or vocalizing
Your innermost pain
That's running through
every single vein.
Loneliness is simply just
hard to explain.
If you try
You start to cry
They feel you imply
They're not good friends
But it's not the whole story
Or even how it bends.
It's so not the point -
At all!

Loneliness is just hard to explain.

It's feeling lost
As if you have no direction
Missing that close connection.

It's feeling empty
Even when there's plenty.

It's feeling numb and naked
When you no longer can fake it.
Loneliness in its singleness
Is hard to explain to the masses,
So you keep burning the matter

To mere dust and ashes.
It's complicated and understated
Concealed with shame -
It's a Silent Game.

Internal Dialogue

The things we tell ourselves

I'm standing in front of the mirror
Frown marking my face
Spreading to my eyes
Trying to disguise the worries
With a smile
Lips falling apart -
Down.

As that frown
expands
I close in
And watch myself carefully
With a dread in my heart
Watching that smile fall apart.
My brain in overdrive
I contemplate the day
What way it will turn
And I say to myself:
"I look tired!
Awful!
Fat!
Feel like crap
Like a failure
With absolutely *no* allure
Of that I am categorically sure."

The pit in my stomach
Grows bigger
Expands to every crevice
Of my insides
Like pesticides
It erodes

And explodes
To something more corrosive
Giving me a dose of heaviness
Making it harder for me
to move forward
And I keep on beating myself up
With words
Internal dialogue
Suffocating in that emotional smog
The darkness
Greyness –
Elusive emptiness?

The words hit me hard
As they continue to beat on
Leaving scars on my soul.
Marred by volatile remark
I let down my guard
Believing the abuse
I choose to tell myself
And I bruise deeply
Feeling the blues
Forgetting it's my personal choice
My own voice
Self-defamation
Continuous stabbing
Turning and twisting
The knife
Draining the elixir of life
Until there's no way back.
All I can do is feel
Leaving no way out to heal

The scars left by my own doing
Have become too deep.

No, that's not how I want things
to end
And I refuse to bend and cave
To the self-abuse
Wanting to turn this day around
Create a new, more gleeful sound
To my inner dialogue.
It's time to flip the switch
And finally cross that bridge.
So, let's try this again!

I'm standing in front of the mirror
Smile spreading across my face
Reaching my sparkly eyes
With nothing to disguise
Lips turning upwards
By the positive words
Forming in my mind
As the happy expression
Expands
My mind finding a spark
Joyfulness
Filling my heart
Every single part of it
Energy bursting through
My veins
Like enticing flames.

I say to myself:
"Hello there gorgeous!
Who really could afford us?
I certainly am precious
Adventurous
I look refreshed
Like I've had the best rest -
I feel so blessed.
Those jeans hug my delightful curves
Sensing my delicate nerves.
It's a good thing!"

I check myself in the mirror
Not looking for error
But beauty -
That magnificent booty.
The cordial words make me feel
so alive -
And I thrive.
I feel good
As I should
'Cause I'm lucky to be here
In the sphere of things
With all the excitement life brings.
I am doing my very best
Fighting through each trying test.
I am kind
Perfectly designed
In tune with my emotions
My own notion of
the potential ambitions
Influential.

I am to others a loyal friend
Who I will always defend.
I am doing my best
Like the rest
Of you all
Sitting in this hall.
Embrace that you are unique
And - trés chic.
Smile through each trial
Work hard at not being in denial
That you've been in the past your own
slanderous, sharp-tongued rival.

I finally feel alive!
I've switched the centralized record
And stored
More positive dialogue
In my internal catalog.
I am a great success
I hereby confess,
A priceless treasure -
Creating never-ending pleasure.

My internal, kinder conversation
- The reinforced commendation -
Will establish much better foundation.
So, from now on and beyond
I will with myself create
a more loving bond.

Paraphrasing

Changing your internal dialogue

Incredible vs. Impossible
Is optimal
Juicy not Overweight,
You debate
Assertive instead of a Bitch
Or a Witch
Empathetic more than Emotional
A Superwoman that's sociable
Nowhere close to Weak
As you're unique.

Beautiful inside and out,
Far from Unattractive
There's no doubt
Exciting vs. Annoying
Your own company you're enjoying.

Always Enough and never Too Much
On that you won't budge
Inspiring rather than Frustrating
Your mind keeps updating
Creative and not Incompetent
Because you're Confident
Yes, a Talented Dramatist.

Thoughtful instead of Numb
Innocently Wise not at all Dumb
More Purposely Relaxed
rather than Lazy
You think it sounds crazy?
Well, I beg to differ.
I'm Honest by a default

With Curves to Die For,
So let's erase all talk of a Big Butt!

The things we tell ourselves
What appeals or repels
Can have a more daunting effect
Make you feel perfect or like a reject
Have poise or recoil.

It's important to be just kind
And not continue to be maligned
By yourself
But change your frame of mind
And leave the negative things behind
Promise not to dig them up
And let them corrupt
Your self-esteem
Or set the theme of
your internal debate
Of all the things you hate
As it takes away your gleam
And ruins your delightful dream.

Yes, the things we tell ourselves
Have a great impact
And dispel a chain reaction
A breakdown of the satisfaction
we find within
That can reconstruct
The most important trust
We can find
Just by being kind -

Yes, kind to ourselves.

The thing that's
So critically vital -
To stop the unhealthy cycle
That's detrimental to your survival -
Is simply to cease being idle:
"Stop the negative talk
Go for a brisk walk.
Don't be afraid to overstock
And unlock
As you keep the sweet-talk
Ongoing around the clock."

That's how you will survive
Keep yourself alive
In full drive
Revive others around you
And simply just hang on and -
Dive fully into the wonder that is
Life!

Lost in Plain Sight

Trying to fit in

Lost
In what sense of the word
Do I feel lost?
Absent
In a moment that's transient?
Adrift
Floating through time and space
The powerful currents unable to resist?
Disoriented
Being secretly, inwardly tormented?
Hidden
From the world
While my story's still unwritten?
Invisible
Because I'm just a part of the typical
Not a true original?

Misplaced
Instead of replaced
Leaving a bad taste in my mouth
That's coated with doubt?
Vanished
As if I'm secretly banished
And famished for love?
Wandering
Aimlessly sauntering
Without destination?
Off-track
Finding no way back
To the road I came from
In denial of who I've truly become?
Being lost

Feeling lost
Is so much more
Than being ignored
Finding yourself off-shore
Or on the floor
Rendered unable to move
Or improve.
It runs so much deeper
Than any surgical procedure
Much more potent
Than not being there in the moment.

It's not having a direction
The loss of real connection
Not finding your purpose
In this ongoing circus
Missing that spark
The hallmark
Of motivation
Sprinkled with a dash
Of indignation
Creating a backlash
Giving you whiplash
As you frantically search
For something
While on the verge
Of tipping over.

Maybe I should just sit and wait
Give in to fate
Let go of all hate
While I continue the debate

with myself
Or until I'm found
Sitting quietly on the ground.

I'm not fretting
Or complaining
Life can sometimes just feel so
damn draining
Especially when it's raining.
But having aspiration
Combined with
Ambition
Simply put,
A focused mission
Or just
A determined goal -
Now, that can truly make you whole.
And then as clear as daylight
You're no longer
Lost in plain sight.

Why Not?

Shedding your fears

Who ever said that I can't?
You
Me
Friends
Or family?
I have,
Me, myself - in the past.
I was way too fast
To blast it out
Afraid of the thing that wouldn't last
Reluctant to fail
So I bailed
And walked the so-called "easy" trail.

But now,
My life's redesigned direction
With more reflection
Has changed a bit.
I refuse to simply sit
With sighing
And just quit
Without trying.

With a full 180
Swayed by perfect hindsight 20/20
The reflexive response will be:
"Why not?"
- A new train of thought.
The act of doing
Inspires pursuing
The things I keep on viewing
As scary

Making me unwary
Instilling in me more confidence -
As a consequence.
It's what makes life worth living
When you keep on giving
To yourself
A string of epic tales
And adventures
As you delve
Head first down that rabbit hole.
Wanna sit on the sidelines
Just sniffing the fine wines
Watching life pass you by
Without even try?

It's time to take a leap in the dark,
To retrieve
Some of the spell-binding spark
Up the ante,
Like an outlawed vigilante
Take life into your own hands,
And make more daring plans
Throw caution to the wind,
And leave doubt behind.
Ergo, I say:
"Why not?"

Detox

Embracing the turning points in life

There comes a time
In your life
That can be hard to define
A time of a great awakening
A time of reckoning
A turning point
Where your body and mind
Are rejoined
And the stars are aligned.

In these moments
Things become ever so clearer
Making your soul shiver
As you recognize the significance.

It's far from being a coincidence
And you know on that occasion,
Not out of any frustration
Or desperation
That you have the chance
To take a firm stance
And change your destination.

All you need is to review
The stops
Have the necessary talks
And simply just -
Detox!

Premiere

Taking the leap

A feeling of exhilaration
Flushes through my body
In the foggy aftermath
Of my decision.
I allowed myself to be freed from
My own created prison
Finally taking control
Of my condition
Realizing it's not causing division
Although it could create
Subsequent suspicion.

Instead, I feel elated
Understand why I waited
Debated
The right move to make
Another risky step to take.
As a result my own worth
became at times
Deflated
At intervals dictated
By other people's assumptions.
I got caught in a whirlwind
Of turmoil until my eyes dimmed
Avoided to act on my own need
Afraid to proceed
But then -
The leap!

It's a new scene
More serene
A brand new chapter

Where I'm the lead actor
Love flowing from the core,
The ultimate factor
Of the seeming drastic change.

It's my life to live
My energy and power to give -
Therefore really
There is nothing to forgive.
I'm finally closing that fiction
That was finished years ago
And now I'm ready to simply
Let go …

I've opened a new book
Taken a closer look
Readjusted the storyline
Cause I really am fine.
I'm starting this exciting new scene
Where everyone is a queen
Or a king
It's a beautiful thing.
The pawns can shine and be seen
Be the main character
in their own story.
There is equal glory
And grace to all
Even after we fall.

Hence,
I invite all who want to take part
And get closer to my heart

To join this new beginning
Keep singing
And grinning
Together as friends
Like we've done in the past -
Time goes by way too fast.

At the risk of sounding like a cliché
I've just chosen a fresh new way
Where I can seize today,
Before time slips through my fingers,
To be free of whatever lingers
In between lines
Of whispers or
Unspoken rhymes.

It's an open invitation
Not separation
But inspiration
To accept a new creation
Vital for my own salvation.

Ergo, I rejoice
In my not so sudden choice.
I feel liberated
Acquitted
No longer on parole
Under control
On the promise of good behavior
Or probation
Subjected to misinterpretation.

I've been released
I've been pardoned
The outline of the new opening scene
Sharpened!

A Transitory Time-Out

Refusing to play games

I feel this weighty stone
Around my neck
Pulling me down -
This heavy pressure
On my chest
Pushing me to drown
Preventing me from rising -
I'm capsizing.

I can't breathe
As the tension underneath
Keeps soaring beneath
The surface
With its own sinister purpose.
My gasps are trapped
At the loaded impact
Arms flail helplessly
And hopelessly
Paying an unsurmountable cost -
The highest price.

The battle lost
I give in to the darkness.
In its eerie stillness
I lie silent -
Nothingness surrounds me
But somehow I feel free.
I hear my own eulogy
In the growing disunity
A tragic elegy
Sounding its own ideology.
For now - succumbing

Is the only way out -
A transitory time-out.
I know with full confidence
- in my current existence -
I will be ready to climb
in due time
And sway another day.

Detachment Response

Watching life pass you by

Ever felt like you don't exist?
That you're simply just a fleeting mist
Crawling ghostly along the surface
Without any particular purpose?
Some might call it acting all casual
Which taps into the rational side
of their own complex mind
Without looking for what's behind
Turning a blind eye
Afraid of the lingering why
That hangs in the air
Like solar flare?

Others might call it being laid-back
Another way to avoid to unpack
What truly drives the withdrawn
Facade I put on
Breathing into it a bit of mystery
When I wistfully
Lift my lips in a surprising smile
That doesn't reach my veiled eyes.

Feeling isolated
In this desolated place
We call life
Removed
In a world that's confused
Severed
From the energy that used to
propel me
I'm now weathered by the things
That made me feel free.

The disconnection is overwhelming
When I keep on dwelling
On the things I should
Not only on what I potentially could
- this thought train is simply
not helping.

Being aloof is a state
I will always hate
But somehow now,
I can relate.
It's frankly just one of those days
Just a temporary phase
In this maze of time
That's hard to define.
I know this all too well
It's this magical spell
That will eventually break
And shake me awake
So I can yet again partake
In the events and affairs
Of my own story
The fabulous future laid before me.

I will soon again,
Not quite sure when,
Bounce back to activity
With all its fascinating futility,
And that sassy spark
Will smother the dark
Before it completely takes over
Or I lose my composure.

This temporary detached state
Is just the usual bump in the road.

I no longer hesitate or
Do a double-take
I snap myself back into survival mode
'Cause I don't want to be late
for my date with Fate.

Muscle Memory

When trauma lingers

My hands are shaking as
Breath hitches in my throat
That sinking feeling reappears
Out of nowhere
As my heart races
Seeing all the faces
Passing by.

I feel I've just run a marathon,
Hope is unexpectedly gone
And I am again becoming withdrawn.

It came as a surprise
Panic in disguise.
I've been happy
And chatty
Okay and fine
Felt myself shine, again
Made new plans
Set goals
Felt excited,
So blissfully delighted.
Mentally I've been doing alright
And the future has been
surprisingly bright.
I'm the best version of me that
I've been in years
Since I began to face and
shed all my fears.

And then …
The blow

The fall
As if I hit another wall.
My mind is confused,
Bemused
At the sudden stumble
As I slowly crumble
And start to fumble in the dark,
once more.
What just happened?

My mind tries to untangle
The perplexing reflexes
But it only deflects
As the puzzlement grows stronger,
The new me is no longer distressed,
Depressed,
Or oppressed.
I am happy!

And yet …

Panic sets in and I fret.
I look around
Look for clues in a sound
If any can be found.
Is there's a hint in the view
I have before me that's new?
Or was it a word poorly considered,
That triggered my undoing
And made me feel withered?
My mood has been fine
As if it's freshly designed

Reprogrammed
Satisfied
Highly elated.

But I forgot
The more enduring memory
Stored in my subconscious
physical directory -
My body.

The trauma I thought I'd figured out
Has yet again showed its ugly snout.
Provoked by an unidentified cause
It's time again to come
to a halt and pause.
With just a bit of self-soothing care
I reflect on all my affairs,
Triggers are a sneaky snare,
As a perfectly wonderful day
Can turn bad and lead you astray.

So, in my resolve to rise and evolve
I do the hard work
Instead of going berserk
Push with vigor
And climb higher as I'm no quitter.
This time I conclude
With a different attitude,
As I fiercely continue to hustle:
"I won't forget the source of
the triggers
Stored in the memory of my muscles."

Wounded by Words

Fighting the tendency

to over-analyze

Words.
The power they contain
Will be branded on your brain.
Inked on your skin
Making your head spin.
The effects they can have leave you
Confused and flustered
Bemused and amused
Bruised and abused.
Powerful indeed
Making your heart bleed
To the point of ruin.

Words.
A different power they have on others
Working like buffers
When there's infliction
Friction
Between friends
They can amend the rift
Be a wonderful gift
Clean the air
Show that you care.

It takes more words to heal
And fewer to make you kneel
To the ground
Break
Even shake.
Being wounded by words
Cuts you deep
Makes you weep and loose sleep.

So be careful how you use them
Don't play dumb and condemn.
Always console and fortify.
Dignify.
Simply do your best
For those you address
Or at least just try
To always unify.

Why Can't You See

Realizing that things are
dysfunctional

You call
I answer the phone
I can sense your tone
But I refuse to fall
Fall for the trick
That you continue to use
On me time and again.

You sigh
I lend a listening ear
Before I used to cry
But now there's not a single tear,
Building up in my eyes.
But I'm right here.
I'm stronger than before
I don't want this anymore.

The emotional distress
I really must confess
That you constantly impose
I feel down to my toes.
Maybe you don't realize
What you do,
How you demoralize me
through and through.
When you call
You want me not to stall
Drop everything I do
It's true.

I'm not exaggerating
Cause if I keep you waiting

I know I will pay a price.
Or is it like rolling the dice?

I say *No*
There's woe
There's no 50/50
You can at times be so shifty.
I say *Yes*
There's a smile on your face.
It's in my internal database
Your reactions
The transactions
The expectations
Frustrations
In our relations.

I want to make you happy
Smile
Joyful
Even for a while.
But I don't want to feel pressured
Measured
Tethered.
Whenever you freeze
I feel like suffocating
It turns into hating
Deflating,
Internal debating.
It's so damn frustrating.

The knot and pain in my core
Almost overtake it all.

Filling every single pore
I want to run for the door.
Why can't you see
What you're doing to me?
I don't know if you realize
That every time you do
Another piece of me dies.

I can see it in your eyes
The tone of your voice
The stiffness of your expression
There's aggression
Oppression.
Depression?
Maybe that's why I'm alert
When you keep on trying to extort
My emotions
My time
My energy.
It puts me in jeopardy.

I wish you could see
Understand how it feels.
And you do
When it is about you.
But why can't you see
The pain I store inside
That you have the key
If you just tried
To ease the pain
Stop the confusion in my brain.
But you don't.

You won't.
You can't?

I've reached the end of the road.
In the nick of time
Before I implode.
I've waited for way too long
And now I'm finally strong
To look you in the eye
Without being shy
Or slowly die.

I'm standing my own ground.
Saying *No* when I need to
And *Yes* when it feels true.
I wish you could see
How hard it's been for me.
How much turmoil it has caused.
Inside.
Like a landslide
It erodes and destroys
Makes noise.

I inhale deeply
Not discreetly
But completely.
I make a determined resolve
Not to dissolve.
But let our relationship evolve.
I will always love you
And me saying *No*
doesn't mean I don't do.

Me saying *No* just means that
I'm through,
Being controlled.
I'm not being cold,
Just bold.
Please understand
I wish you could see
I wish you could hear my plea.
I love you
But this is my breakthrough.
My love for you won't ever change.
But the control I need to exchange
For something greater.
Get rid of the emotional dictator.

So, this is what I long for
More and more,
That you can let go
And allow yourself to glow,
Simply just grow,
You know?
Then maybe you could see
The true person within me
Let go of the control
And finally, allow yourself
to become whole.

Kiss. My. Butt.

Fighting anxiety

You entered my life
Without invitation
Like a wrecking ball
Creating havoc -
Devastation.
With a forceful hand
You put on the pressure.
Suffocating
Obliterating
Frustrating
My heart kept racing.
Stomach dropping
Hands shaking
I felt like almost breaking.

"Get out," I say.
"Get out," I pray.
But you linger -
Refuse to let go.
Squeeze harder.
My spirit smashing
I feel the crash
Heart shattered
My courage is battered
With no way out
From this emotional drought.
I close my eyes
Count to ten
Revive a determined soul
Reinforce the joy for life
Wave away sadness and strife.
I need to fight

Toward the light.
There's no more room for you,
Believe me it's beyond true.
In my existence, there's
No more space
No place
No spot
No lot.

A final step,
I do the prep
I stand firm and tall
To face you head-on after all.
Knuckles white at my side
Ready for the fight.
"Get out," I howl, I hiss
Repeating myself with gutsy bliss.
With force and fire
I push back
I push hard.
I promise to never tire.

There's no more falling,
And I keep calling:
"Anxiety! Fear!
Just see if I care.
I finally trust my gut.
So, go ahead,
And Kiss. My. Butt."

Numbness

When your energy level is low

I am okay
That's all I need to say.
But truth be told
The fire
Desire
And spark
Have gone dark.
Numbness is all around
Just as I come down from the high
And crash to the rough ground
Whispering wistfully:
"Goodbye."

A Little Fairytale

When you allow fear

to hold you back

Once upon a time
There was a tiny little bird
That was a victim of a callous crime
Locked up in a confining cage
Which filled him with ravishing rage.
Then on one searing summer's day
Or was it in moderate May
The door of the cage opened.
The little bird saw this blessed break
And knew his life was seriously
at stake

He flew away
And no longer felt at bay.
He explored the land,
Stones & the sand
Tulips & trees
Birds & the bees
But the world out there was too big
For an innocent bird to explore -
For it to survive.
So, back to the cage he flew
In the early morning dew.

Exiled No More

Participating in life again

How to work through pain
Any pain
Internal or otherwise
Your external disguise?
It's one of the bigger question
Leaving you open to
many suggestions.
You cut yourself open
Open wide
Begin to confide
In someone
Anyone
A trusted friend
That can comprehend
The ache you carry inside.
You pour out your heart
Fall apart
Allow it to bleed -
It's bittersweet.

You write it all down
Express yourself with words
Spoken
Or
Written
- Words in herds.
Your tears gush down your cheeks
Like creeks
Wetting the paper
As the ink smudges
The terms you've scribbled.
They are filled with your pain,

Your internal refrain.
Can you feel it?
Do you sense it?

It's all mine
And - It could be yours
Of course
Whenever you feel out of sorts
Or the need to share
With your own flair.
But that's yours to tell
Not mine to yell -
Or reveal
How you truly feel.

I need the words
The pain to stay
On the paper
Way off my radar
Leave it there
Like some twisted love affair
Hanging in the air -
I don't want them crawling back
For yet another merciless attack.

Expressions of the inner turmoil
Is out there for the world to see
A daring decree
That keeps me naked and bare
To be witnessed.
It's not bitterness

That's being revealed
- Or unsealed.

It's vulnerability
In my shakiness
Knowing that not everywhere
Is a safe space
A soft spot to fall -
A harmless haven that acts
As your protective wall.
That is why I fall back on my feet -
And retreat -
Remove myself from the equation
Candidly learning my own limitation.
I need to be careful
And take care of my body,
My soul,
Until I become whole again
And can maintain a realistic balance.

That is the gist
On my checklist.
But I need time
Time - that's mine.
The words bleeding through the pages
Endless pages of confessions
Is the pain piercing my skin
Hacking at my heart
Stabbing my soul,
Over and over -
Until there's nowhere to hide.

No more!
I want to heal
I know life won't feel real
If I don't show zeal
And do the heavy lifting -
I sense the withering shadows shifting.
I want to be restored again
Bring back
The exiled me,
The person I know that's there
Free from hollow fear.

The courageous girl
And fearless fighter
The tenacious lassie
And daring damsel.
She's still in there
- Somewhere -
Fighting to get out
From her ebbing hideout
Fighting to not give up
Letting out a triumphant shout
Jousting for her own life.

I don't want her to disappear
That is why I'm still here
And I will get her back
As I contend through the pitch black
Making a heroic comeback.
I will be me again
I will with 100% guarantee
In the fullest degree

Return -
From exile.

Turning Over

a New Leaf

Appreciating

the aha moments in life

I am angry.
I am pissed.
A rage I didn't know I contained
And retained
Had gone amiss.
There's built-up frustration
Sensation,
Growing from within.
Where do I begin?

I've been holding back
Scared of the feedback.
The judgment and scrutiny
Fearing uprising and mutiny.
From myself.
From all of them.
It's made me numb
But beneath the surface
I'm neurotically nervous
Of bearing my soul
Trying to feel whole
Contemplating a new role.

Realizing and recognizing
That no one person
Can make you feel a certain way
Can make your day gray
Can force someone to stay
Or even lead you astray.

I have the power
Brainpower

Willpower
- Simply just the power
To control my own ending.
No more time
I will keep spending
Defending
My actions and vows.
Some interest they arouse.

I want people of positivity around
And air of negativity
Nowhere to be found.
Having friends that build up
And never stop
Spreading devotion.
Being loving
Intuitive
Showing affection
And showing initiative -
That is my new direction.

Positive feelings
And healthy dealings.
Stable friendships
Not the Apocalypse.
It might sound dramatic
But it's just being pragmatic
When you take your power back
Before things turn black.
When you protect your heart -
It's just being smart.

When you learn to say
Yes,
Or *No*
It will help you to grow.
Recognizing you have a choice
Even rejoice.
What's so wrong with that?

Okay, let's cut the crap
Get to the nitty gritty
And don't even try to be witty.
It truly is a real thing
In this boxing ring called -
Life.
The power is yours
To open countless doors
To show you variety
In society
Sans all the anxiety.
You can be you
A part of the crew
For someone *the* super glue.
It takes courage and confidence
To think without consequence
Within clear-cut boundaries
- Of course -
Get advice from the right source.

You start to wonder
Whether it's responsible
Or not.
Too volatile

Or impossible.
But it's just life
No biggie
It can at times get sticky.
That's just it.
It's just life
And it needs to be lived.
I can feel the excitement
Rise from within,
As I slap on a wide-eyed grin.

In any case,
Back to business
And release that stiffness
In your back and neck.
What the heck?
Today, I say,
With absolutely no regret or grief -
I'm turning over a new leaf.

intention of the mind

Creating your own story

hesitation
hampers happiness
inhibits inventiveness
cripples creativity

curiosity
establishes originality
designs dynamics
paints a palette

that's when your life
turns into a story
a script
a word-puzzle

write it well
avoid over-editing
and cling to optimism

Polly Prose

ACKNOWLEDGMENTS

From the bottom of my heart, I want to thank my friends and family, and all those who unknowingly supported me in starting to write again and finally take the step to self-publish my first book of poetry.

You all know who you are.

I also want to thank my favorite café around the corner that provided me with a cozy environment to create and write. Brainstorming while sipping on your favorite coffee paired with a warm and crunchy croissant is the perfect setting.

Special thanks to my sister and cousin, who were instrumental in helping me decide on the style of my book cover.

Polly Prose

The making of this collection has been a
fun process, and the support I've received
nothing short of amazing.

I love you all!

ABOUT THE AUTHOR

Polly Prose is a poet from Reykjavik, Iceland, with a fresh voice. And *Echoes of Silence* is her debut collection of poetry.

For years she has dreamt of becoming a published writer and finally made the leap with this intimate collection.

Polly's work has been published in poetry anthologies online and in print.

She is currently living in Copenhagen and exploring the poetry scene locally.

You can find more of her work on Instagram @PollyProse and www.authorpollyprose.com.

Keep an eye out for more of her works in the future.

To all lovers of the spoken and written word,

Thank you for stopping by!

COMING SOON…

Cobwebs by Polly Prose.

A little appetizer:

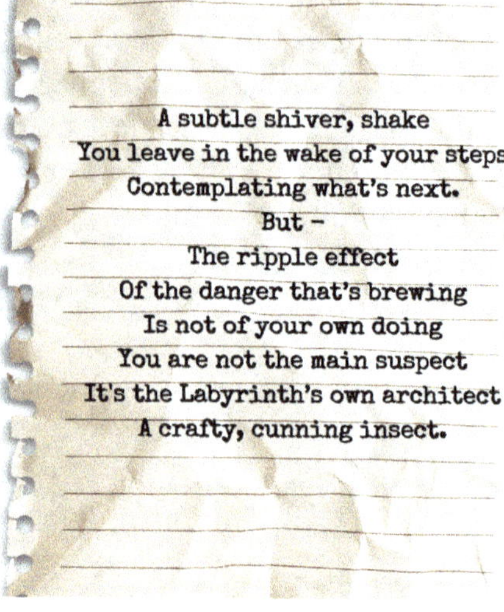

9 788879 751410 8